TRANSCENDING AUTISM THROUGH YOGA AND MEDITATION:
AN AUTISM OWNER'S MANUAL

KEVIN WOOLDRIDGE

Copyright © 2023 Kevin Wooldridge

All rights reserved.

No part of this book may be used or reproduced in any manner whatsoever without written permission except in the case of brief quotations embodied in critical articles and reviews.

ISBN: 979-8-9894928-0-0

DEDICATION

To my dear friends Penny Walsh, Kara Lough, Frank Tennyson, Dave Scarborough, Terra Vajcner, and my family members Joan Wooldridge, Kenny Wooldridge, Ryan Grell, Gale Williams, Andrew Wooldridge, and Heather Williams. You have all contributed to this book, whether directly or indirectly, by sharing your love and patience with me for all these years.

Also to Tanisha Brown and Jenny So, two friends whose questions inspired me to write this book.

ACKNOWLEDGMENTS

This book would not have been possible without the ongoing support and encouragement of Penny Walsh, my best friend, who always knows how to bring out the best in me, in spite of myself most of the time. Thanks to Terra Vajcner and Joanne Yates for reading the manuscript and making suggestions that helped me choose the best words to convey my thoughts. Thanks to Don Bruns and Rick Kaempfer for offering their keen insights on how to write and publish a book.

CONTENTS

INTRODUCTION	1
PART ONE – MY EXPERIENCE OF AUTISM	5
1. How An Autistic Person Shows Up to The World	6
2. The Late 1960's – Baby Kevin	9
3. The 1970's – Elementary School	10
4. The 1980's – Radio, and Rock and Roll	14
5. Junior High	16
6. High School	18
7. University of Arkansas	22
8. DJ Kevin Kelly	23
9. My First Girlfriend	26
10. The 1990's – So I Got to be a Radio Star	26
11. How My Future Father-in-law Introduced Me to My Future Wife	28
12. The World's Most Famous Beach	30
13. The 2000's – Ohio	31
14. Coworkers	31
15. Kids and Autism	32
16. The 2010's – Expanding Horizons	33

17. Exploring With My Photography Group	33
18. New York, New York	34
19. Swimming Lessons	35
20. Dad's Passing	35
21. First Concert Alone	36
22. The Law of Attraction	36
23. Meditation Family	38
24. Yoga Family	38
25. My Autism Diagnosis	39
26. First Concert Trip to Chicago Alone	40
27. First Movie Alone	41
28. Moving Day 2016	41
29. Adult Relationships	42
PART TWO – SELF HELP GUMBO	**45**
30. Yoga	46
31. Meditation	48
32. Mindfulness	49
33. Journaling	51
34. Counseling	52
35. Peer Support	52

36.	Physical Activity	53
37.	Spend Time Outdoors in Nature	53
38.	Gratitude	54
39.	Positive Self-talk	55
40.	Affirmations	57
41.	Decluttering	58
42.	Posture	58
43.	Communication	59
44.	Choose Your Friends Wisely	59
45.	The Cumulative Effect	62

PART THREE – THE SWEETNESS OF MOMENTS   **63**

46.	My Current Experience of Life	64
47.	The 2020's – Pandemic Driving	64
48.	The Atlantic Ocean	65
49.	Moving Day 2020	66
50.	Swimming and Kayaking	66
51.	Final Thoughts	67

INTRODUCTION

Have you ever felt like no matter what you try to do, your life never gets better? Like you are stuck repeating the same negative patterns over and over again? I spent the first 40 years of my life making choices that left me feeling unhappy and unfulfilled, trying to fit in and feel normal. In an effort to find my way, I consulted friends and family, took college courses in leadership, and read self-help books. Nothing seemed to help me figure out why I couldn't make good decisions for myself.

Then, my child was diagnosed with Autism Spectrum Disorder. I decided to try and learn more, so I went out and bought a book about autism. While reading that book, I saw a little bit of my son in the author's stories, but I saw a lot more of myself.

Fortunately, at the time, I was seeing a therapist for relationship issues whose primary practice was focused on children with autism. Following several lengthy discussions with my therapist, I was finally diagnosed as an adult with autism.

The diagnosis wasn't the end of my search for answers, but a new beginning. I was now able to look back at my life with a fresh understanding of why I made certain decisions in my life and always felt like an outsider. Over time, I finally began to understand that my real quest and goal was to learn how to love myself as I am and to live an enjoyable and fulfilling life.

This book is divided into three sections: My Experience of Autism, Self Help Gumbo, and the Sweetness of Moments. Here's how that happened.

One of my Facebook friends asked me in late March 2019 to

write a few sentences to explain what it's been like for me to live with autism, as she had been recently diagnosed also. I thought to myself there's no way to condense this down to a few sentences when I'm trying to write an entire book about it. She needs an entire autism owner's manual! With that thought, the proverbial light bulb went off over my head, leading to the subtitle of the book. I debated whether the owner's manual should be a clinical explanation of what autism is, but decided to instead simply tell my own story. There are plenty of resources that describe autism in general. So, the first part of the book - My Experience of Autism - is an owner's manual explanation of what MY life has been like living on the spectrum.

The second part of the book is called Self Help Gumbo. When I tried to figure out how yoga and meditation contributed to my healing, I realized that they worked together, along with several other things I was doing, like forcing myself to do things outside my comfort zone and decluttering my home and my life. I had recently enjoyed some Cajun food, and realized that I had mixed together all these self-help modalities, just like a tasty Cajun gumbo.

Most people will say that autism manifests itself as a lack of ability to feel or express empathy with others. The Unitarian minister who helped me grieve my father's death had a slightly different way of explaining it. He thought I was making faulty assumptions about what other people were thinking. He urged me to begin any new relationship by telling the woman that I would need clear feedback on the relationship, because my assumption making mechanism is broken. To illustrate, a woman once told me she needed more space, which I agreed to give. But later on, I realized I had no idea how much space she needed, and I felt like I was already giving her plenty. I used the "faulty assumptions" definition for a long time, but it never seemed to fit perfectly. After ten years of reflection, I believe I finally found a better way to describe autism.

The best explanation of my experience with autism was given to me in August 2019 by my meditation guide, Frank Tennyson. Earlier that day, I'd been talking with a friend who mentioned riding horses. I recalled that I'd only ridden a horse one time, back in 1988. I had been filling out a job application at my hometown radio station, when I struck up a conversation with the cute girl sitting next to me, then asked her on a date. She was also filling out an application for the job. Neither of us got the job, but she agreed to a date! She invited me to her family's farm, where we rode her horse around a field, then returned to the barn, sat on a bale of hay, and kissed a little bit. My faded memory of the afternoon is that she had a Disney obsession, and talked a lot about Disney characters. I thought she was weird and she probably thought I was too. Because of my autism, I probably talked about music a lot. Or, more likely, I didn't know what to say to her and didn't talk much at all. Chances are, she was as nervous as I was, and talking about cartoon characters was her way of handling the anxiety. Anyway, there was no second date.

Later that night, that friend and I went to meditation at Frank's house, and out of the blue he started talking about autism. He said autism was "the inability to experience the sweetness of moments." Right then and there it hit me… that girl on the horse going on and on about Disney characters was sharing two of her passions with me: riding her beloved horse, and talking about her favorite Disney characters. And the only thing that resonated with me in the actual moment was kissing her on the bale of hay! I totally missed the sweetness of the moment! Which is probably the actual reason I never saw her again. The only reason I realized all this during that meditation is that I'd put in several years of work on myself through healing modalities like yoga and meditation.

The third part of the book owes its name to Frank's fateful words about the Sweetness of Moments. I believe that if I tell you what my life was like before my diagnosis, then tell you how I overcame the diagnosis, I should also detail what a life can be like once you move beyond the things that hold you back. The lessons I have learned could be useful to so many other people, and not just people with autism. These healing modalities can benefit anyone who feels stuck in life! Once I realized all these things, I knew that I had to write this book and share my experiences with the world.

My challenge to you once you've finished reading this is to lay out a plan to create and use your own Self-Help Gumbo (which could include a yoga and meditation practice) to open up and feel the Sweetness of Moments.

PART ONE

MY EXPERIENCE OF AUTISM

1 HOW AN AUTISTIC PERSON SHOWS UP TO THE WORLD

You may not believe it if you met me for the first time today, but I have been diagnosed as an adult with autism. Many people have assumptions about people with autism. They think we are socially handicapped, awkward, unhappy, or shy. It's not easy to transcend the social limitations that others place on us. Not to mention the limitations we place on ourselves.

As a child, I was described as shy. True to form, I adopted that description as part of my biography, clinging tightly to it until my mid-forties. But the word "shy" is deceiving. Truth be told, I tried to interact with other children, but my social skills weren't great. If you try to be social, but the other kids ignore or make fun of you, eventually you probably withdraw from trying. That's the point where others label you "shy." The adults must know what they are talking about, right? So, I believed that I was "shy."

It's often difficult for us to fit in because autism affects the decision-making parts of a person's brain. So, how was I able to eventually learn how to enjoy a fulfilling life with autism? The short answer is that I learned how to find and maintain meaningful relationships with individuals and groups who share my interests. In fact, I've done a lot of work over the last ten years to find social situations with supportive people that I both enjoy and find comfortable.

To understand my journey, you will need to know where I started. The best place for us to begin is with an explanation of what autism looks like. At least, this is what it looked like in MY life. Your mileage may vary.

I should mention this also… If you think you may have autism and want an official diagnosis, it's best to see a professional such as a therapist or psychologist who specializes in autism. To be diagnosed, you must have a certain combination of social impairments and restricted/repetitive behaviors, which I'll talk about briefly. There are seven on the list. You must exhibit some of the first three (which are the social pieces) plus at least two of the last four (which are the behavioral pieces).

For different reasons, it can be difficult to diagnose both children and adults. Some or all of the behaviors/impediments may not become evident in a young child as they develop until social demands exceed their social capacities. On the other hand, some adults learn masking strategies that hide some of their symptoms. There's a lot to unpack here!

In true autistic fashion, I spent three months stuck at this exact spot while writing the book, overanalyzing how to move forward and explain my experience with being on the spectrum! I finally realized that it's my story, not a diagnostic tool, so it doesn't matter how I tell the story.

I chose not to get too far into the weeds on terminology, because I might have spent another year or two trying to get everything perfect. It's just a book, and just my thoughts. Please don't take it more seriously than necessary. I also use the terms autistic and person with autism interchangeably.

You've probably never heard the nervous system explained like this before, but it's crucial to understanding what it's like to be on the spectrum. For all of us humans, our sensory organs (skin, nose, eyes, ears, tongue) generate electrical impulses based on what they detect around us. These impulses are carried to the brain by nerve cells, and are then decoded by the brain. The capacity of these nerves could be compared to a water hose. Most people have a capacity like a fire hose, easily handling a deluge of sensory inputs. Someone like me on the spectrum has a capacity more like a garden hose. When the world around an autistic person is soft and quiet, their garden hose can carry all the current stimuli to the brain. But take them to a crowded mall or a rock concert, and the garden hose quickly becomes a bottleneck. A lot of the stimuli gets left out of the messages sent to the brain. That person just can't deal with everything going on around them.

Then, it gets more interesting. Most neurotypical people have brains that can quickly process all the stimuli they are experiencing as they go about their daily routine. Someone with autism is only able to process things in their mind at a fraction of the speed of the average person, but their sensory perception is far more sensitive, so that person is feeling several times the feelings of an average person. Our brains get so overwhelmed that it is hard to just be and feel present.

Meditation, yoga, and mindfulness were the keys to beginning my improvement. They helped me to center and focus more inward, therefore allowing me to tune out some of the excess stimulation around me. My brain isn't processing any faster now, but there's less stuff to process, so I'm no longer feeling overwhelmed these days.

This is important, so I want to say it again. Your symptoms might not match mine. See a qualified therapist if you want to obtain a diagnosis and explore other coping mechanisms. It is difficult to self-diagnose because many conditions have overlapping symptoms. Also, don't discount the healing modalities if your experience with autism is different than mine. The healing modalities I will share later in the book will generate results for nearly anyone who desires healing, regardless of where one might be on the spectrum.

Allow me to add a disclaimer before I begin sharing my story. I am 99% sure that these stories happened exactly the way I remember them. If someone else was involved in a story and remembers something differently, then there's a chance they might be correct. Or maybe we are both partially correct. Remember the old anecdote which states there are three sides to any story. There's my side, your side, and somewhere in the middle lies the truth. And memory is a tricky thing.

2 THE LATE 1960'S – BABY KEVIN

I was born in Arkansas during the spring of 1968 and adopted by my parents at the age of three months. My earliest memory is of Christmas 1969. I was 21 months old. I was sitting on the floor at my aunt and uncle's house, playing with a toy Jack in the Box they had just given me. The room seemed so big since I was looking at it from a toddler's perspective. So far, I haven't searched for my birth parents. My dad died almost twelve years ago now, around the time of my diagnosis. I never got the chance to ask him if he noticed autistic traits in me as a child.

3 THE 1970'S – ELEMENTARY SCHOOL

Around the time when I was 5 years old, my dad would take me to one of the two barber shops for a haircut, then across the street to the coffee shop. Every time we went into the coffee shop, I would ask Dad for a nickel so I could play a disco song that was popular at the time, "Rock the Boat" by Hues Corporation, on their jukebox. I didn't realize it at the time, but patterns and rituals are important for me and many other people on the spectrum.

The first time I realized I was different from other kids was in that coffee shop. One day after receiving a haircut, we crossed the street to the coffee shop. And this wasn't a hipster coffee shop, it was a small-town Arkansas coffee shop with a few old men hanging out. Someone noticed that I had picked up a newspaper and started reading it. He asked if I was really understanding what I was reading. So, I began to read the article out loud. I can't remember exactly what the men said next, but they seemed impressed that a young kid could read so well. I remember wondering what all the fuss was about, because I didn't realize I was doing anything unusual. I learned to read by watching PBS. Old TV shows like Sesame Street, Electric Company, and 3-2-1 Contact taught me all the letters and how to read. Armed with that knowledge, I devoured every book and newspaper I could find.

Later on, when I was in second grade, they let us read at our own pace through a reading program called the SRA Reading Laboratory. I blew through the whole thing (including the third-grade books) and they didn't know what to do with me for the remainder of the school year. I didn't care how they solved the problem; I just wanted more books to read.

I was good at learning, but not good at socializing. My memories of kindergarten are mostly of watching Sesame Street on a small TV on top of a rolling cart and using finger paints to make art. I don't remember any social interactions with the other kids. Not a single one. I remember feeling a bit lonely, but I didn't seem to be able to make friends easily.

At some point in the early 70s, Mom took me to the city pool for swimming lessons. She says I lasted two weeks. The only other thing she remembers about it now was that I didn't learn how to swim. My only memory is of being pushed into the pool and crying. Afterwards, I had no interest in getting back into the water. Most autistic people have issues with sensory overstimulation, and the combination of being unsupported by anything under my feet along with the sudden immersion in water and the distractions of other kids swimming and making noise was just too much for me.

I have fond memories from elementary school of several of my teachers and a few of the kids. The funny thing about this is, if you asked them today, they'd probably have positive memories of me. It wasn't like people hated me or anything like that, it's just that most people weren't super close to me.

I remember getting to leave the classroom to beat the erasers. Kids today will never know that joy. We had green or black chalkboards on the front wall of each classroom. The teacher wrote things on the board using white chalk. Naturally, the teacher needed a way to clean the words or numbers off the chalkboard at the end of class. That tool was an eraser, made of felt. From time to time, the erasers needed to be cleaned of all the chalk buildup. A good student was usually nominated by the teacher to go outside and "beat the erasers" on the sidewalk to knock off all the chalk. I remember one time I was sent out with a friend to beat the erasers. We walked to the far side of the playground, where we found something to beat them on. We must have stayed out too long, because the teacher finally came looking for us. I really enjoyed those mostly solitary moments. In the classroom, I was always having self-conscious thoughts, worrying what the other kids were thinking about me. Wondering what they thought of my clothes or my hair or what I said if the teacher called on me to answer a question. Anytime I could escape the classroom and the company of others, I welcomed the alone time.

I was a big fan of the TV show Star Trek. It shouldn't come as any surprise that my favorite character was Mr. Spock. His logic and use of big words like "affirmative" appealed to me. I also really liked super heroes, like Superman, Green Lantern, and Batman. I wanted to be like them, to have powers beyond normal people. Looking back, I think I mostly wanted people to like me and respect me, since I never felt like I fit in.

In elementary school, there were a few boys who picked on me, or bullied me. The funny thing is, I remember being bullied, but only a few of the actual events. I remember some name calling, because I was skinny and not athletic. One day a kid pushed me down in the dirt on the playground, then he grinned at me while leaning over and making a big deal about extending his hand to help me up. I had finally had enough, and sensed an opportunity. He was slightly off balance, so I grabbed his hand and pulled as hard as I could. He flew over me, and landed on the ground himself. I was proud that I stood up for myself. Our friends laughed at the other kid taking a fall, and he never messed with me again.

One thing I've noticed about having autism is that once I get in the habit of doing something, it's hard to stop. One year, our homeroom teacher let us know that we could do written and oral reports on any topic to get a few extra points added on our grade at the end of the quarter. I probably didn't need to worry about my grade, but I liked researching and learning things, so I started doing reports. Every night when I went home, I would open up one of the books in our encyclopedia set and read an article about one of the planets. Then I would write a report and take it to school the next day and present it to the class. Once I finished writing everything about the planets, I moved on to other scientific topics. I probably read half the encyclopedia!

After several weeks of presenting a daily report, I went to school one morning and felt embarrassed when I realized I had forgotten to write my report the previous night. Out of habit, the teacher called on me to stand in front of the class to start our school day with my report. I wasn't able to tell her that I hadn't done one, so I just stood there without anything to say until she realized what was happening and told me to sit down. I still remember blushing with embarrassment. One of my fellow students then asked the teacher how many extra points I had earned with all those reports. She said she didn't know, but my friend insisted on calculating my grade. Finally, the teacher gave in and presented her grade book to my friend. After a few minutes of calculation, he announced to the class that my grade was over 300%! I wasn't allowed to do any more extra points reports.

Needless to say, given the option of socializing with other children or adults, I would gravitate to the adults most of the time. This happened whether it was at school or family gatherings. Whenever I was allowed, I'd stay in the classroom during recess and talk with my teacher instead of going outside to play with the other kids. I'd do the same thing at our family gatherings. I'd stay closer to my parents or some relative from their generation instead of playing with the other kids. I would later learn that this is a normal autistic trait. The other kids weren't able to understand and adapt to my quirky behavior. Adults are better equipped to interact with someone autistic without making them feel unwelcome. So, I hung around the adults because I felt more accepted.

4 THE 1980'S – RADIO, AND ROCK AND ROLL

One place I never felt out of place was sitting in my swing in our backyard, listening to the radio all day. I used to wake up during the summer of 1980 and go outside with my radio to listen to the Ray Lincoln show on KAAY. Sometimes I would wake up as early as six AM. The morning dew would make my bare feet feel a little cold as I walked through the grass from the carport to the swing set. I'd often get a sunburn from sitting in the swing all day. The reason I didn't like to be inside was, the TV would often be on, causing static on my AM radio. In the early 80s, the stations I listened to were mostly far away AM stations like KAAY from Little Rock or WLS from Chicago. Static was a bad thing.

KAAY had a slogan in 1980: "Entertainment for the Eighties!" and it made me aware that for the first time in my conscious life, I was entering a new decade. I had just turned 12, so I was entering a new phase of my life as well. I was discovering how much I loved music and how much I wanted to know more about girls. But listening to the radio was my main source for social interaction. Listening to my radio heroes required very little effort on my part. Those radio personalities became very important to me.

I knew other kids, but I never felt super close to anyone around this age. I didn't know why I didn't seem to fit in. We all had similar cultural experiences. We only had a handful of TV stations and radio stations. So, we all watched the same shows and mostly listened to the same music. There were two movie screens - the drive-in theater a block from my house and the "walk-in movie" in an old theater just behind the old post office. The biggest difference between any of us, looking back, was how much money your family had and which church your family belonged to. Most people didn't consider themselves "members" of a church, they "belonged" to the particular church. Yes, we were that isolated and rural. The two closest towns with decent shopping or cultural events were Little Rock AR and Monroe LA, both two hours away by car. I longed for experiences that I saw in movies or on TV. I wanted to see New York City and southern California, but all I got was pine trees and dirt roads.

5 JUNIOR HIGH

Entering seventh grade in the fall of 1980 was a difficult transition for me. Up through the sixth grade, we started every day in homeroom. We spent most of the day with that same teacher, who we got to know very well. We were also allowed to finish any homework that we didn't do the night before. The only deviance in that routine was once a week PE class or our afternoon math class. In seventh grade, everything quickly changed. I had a different teacher every hour! At the end of each hour, a bell would ring, and we had five minutes to gather up our books and move them from one room to another. And I might even need to squeeze a bathroom break into those five minutes. Out in the narrow hallway, I had to navigate my way through a noisy, moving crowd of other kids who were quickly moving towards their next class. This was very upsetting to me. Too much stimuli. Plus, I wasn't used to having to learn where so many classrooms were located all at once. Since I had more limited interactions with each teacher, I didn't become comfortable with them easily, causing me to experience a lot of stress and social pressure. I always felt self-conscious, like everyone knew that I was feeling so out of place. Surely, they must notice it. Being autistic and caught up in my own thoughts, I didn't realize that I wasn't alone in those feelings.

To make things worse, every teacher assigned homework every night! I wasn't used to having this much homework. Up until this point, I already knew most things they were covering in class. Seventh grade was the turning point where the teachers began introducing material that was new to me.

Over the summer of 1980, my newfound love of radio and

music caused me to develop a new routine. I had begun listening to the radio during all my free time. Homework didn't fit into this new obsession. I couldn't focus on homework for any length of time, because I wasn't interested in most of the subject matter. My grades began to suffer, because for the first time, the teachers were presenting material that I hadn't already learned on my own. But I was steadily learning new music.

Most kids can roll with the punches and adapt to the changes fairly quickly. But I was different. I continued to feel overwhelmed with the flow of kids through the hallways between classes, the homework load, and the awkwardness of trying to approach and meet people well beyond my high school years.

My eighth-grade algebra teacher remembered a few years ago that I couldn't wait for the opportunity to get into her office and work on one of the TRS-80 computers. She said it was like a compulsion or obsession for me. If they had known about autism back then, I would have been diagnosed during my junior high years for sure. One of my special interests was mathematical patterns like origami. I would often get extra credit for these research projects. I continued to spend a lot of time researching interesting topics of my own choosing. To this day, I still have issues focusing on work tasks that I find mundane or boring. Unfortunately, it's hard to get "extra credit" at work for ignoring your assignments and doing your own thing.

I finally became aware that I wasn't the only socially awkward kid when I was in junior high. There were a couple of kids who were actually more socially awkward than me. Looking back now, I realize they probably were on the autism spectrum also. In those days, they just seemed quirky. Seeing how people perceived them gave me an idea of how people might see me. I just wasn't quite as quirky. I wanted to be popular, like some of the other kids were, but I didn't know how.

I enjoyed watching comedians on TV and I noticed they almost always had their audiences laughing. I would sometimes learn one of their jokes and try telling it at school. Sometimes this made people laugh. One time, we were on the bus to some out-of-town trip, and someone yelled out asking some stupid question that I can't exactly remember. I jumped out of my seat and said something crazy to try and impress the girl sitting next to me. Unfortunately, my comment embarrassed her, and she got up and moved to another seat, and I was by myself for the next hour of the trip. One of many instances of failing to consider the consequences of something I decided to say. I would blame a faulty brain to mouth filter for years, but the true root of the issue was not being able to put myself in someone else's shoes and think how my words would impact them. I was beginning to find myself in even more diverse social situations that I just wasn't prepared to handle.

6 HIGH SCHOOL

One of the most important lessons I learned in high school was to not tilt at every windmill. If you don't understand that reference, it's ok. Neither did I. After all these years, I still haven't read Don Quixote.

We had a teacher who was very polarizing. You either loved her or hated her. She'd been teaching for so many years, the way she treated you was based on whether or not she liked your older siblings (or parents) when she had them in class! If you attended her church, then she usually liked you. I was the first (and only) member of my family to have her, so she had to make up her mind solely based on interactions with me. And she wasn't a fan because I didn't do a great job with my homework.

This teacher would insult kids and call them "stupid" in front of the rest of the class. I think she considered that to be motivational. Kids would leave the room and mutter "bitch" under their breath as they entered the hallway.

Her classroom had a chalkboard mounted on the wall, but for reasons unknown, she also had a freestanding chalkboard propped up in the chalk tray that she preferred to use. When she became agitated for some reason, she would write notes and press the chalk into the board so hard, the board would start to tip forward. Occasionally, someone would say after class they thought it was going to tip over and fall on her head.

One day she came in and was in a particularly angry mood. Someone made a sound while she was writing on the board. She stopped writing, turned around and glared at us as she prepared to speak. "Some of you people don't think I'm a good teacher. Tell me one thing I could do to be a better teacher." Dead silence. "Come on. Any one of you." Still dead silence. "I thought so. I know some of you go out of here and call me a bitch. And it's true. I AM a bitch. And one day if any of you make it to college, you'll thank me for being a bitch!" She grabbed a yardstick and pointed it at the student sitting in the front row closest to her, called his name and asked, "Am I a bitch?!?" With a look of terror on his face he sat straight up in his desk and said, "Yes ma'am, you sure are!" She yelled, "Thank you!" and smashed the yardstick on the top of his desk, breaking it into two pieces.

She walked back over to the chalkboard, put the remnants of the ruler back in the chalk tray, and turned around and flashed us a rare smile. Then the bell rang to signal the end of class. We sat very still until she dismissed us.

I had study hall next, so I went to a staff member and related the story of what just happened. She seemed a little puzzled, but said that the teacher had just been through some teacher training, and maybe she was in fact actually seeking constructive criticism. She suggested I go out into the study hall and quietly ask if anyone had some constructive suggestions for how that teacher could better instruct her class. If I weren't autistic, I would have realized that my teacher's question about how she could be a better teacher was a rhetorical question, because she thought she was the perfect teacher. But since I AM autistic, I walked back out into the study hall and took out my notebook.

I started with the people who sat at my table. Then went to the others. Everyone in the study hall took time to write a suggestion in my notebook. As I was collecting suggestions, I missed something important that was spontaneously occurring. When many of my fellow students finished writing their suggestions, they left the study hall area and went to different classes to tell other kids what I was doing. Before long, I noticed there was a line of people waiting to write suggestions. (I counted the suggestions later that night. 120 kids had written a suggestion. That was one third of the entire student body!) At the end of study hall, I took my notebook to the staff member. When she saw the number of pages of suggestions, she seemed a bit startled. She asked me to take it home and edit and condense it down to a single page that could be typed and placed in the teacher's mailbox. I fulfilled the request, and she placed the letter in the teacher's mailbox the next day.

The following day, the teacher read the letter and was furious. I could tell she was angry, but she didn't say a word about it. One of my friends was out sick that day, and for some reason, she assumed it was him. The next day, she asked him to remain after class, and yelled at him. It took him a little while to convince her that he had no idea what she was talking about. Fifteen minutes into my next class, she barged in the door and declared that she needed a word with me. We walked out into the hall and the whole class listened to her yell at me. I don't remember what she said, but nobody said a word when I came back in and sat down.

A couple of years later, one of my former teachers was talking with me about this and a couple of other situations where I protested an injustice against a fellow student. He told me, "You don't have to tilt at every windmill." Read Don Quixote if you want to understand the reference. Then please explain it to me. The moral of the story according to my teacher was, pick and choose your battles. He said I would get through life easier if I let more things slide. I have to think though, that I did make a difference in this case. The next year, they hired a new teacher and gave him the angry teacher's favorite class. She retired the following year.

If you are wondering how this ties into my expression of autism, I think if I hadn't been autistic, I would have realized all the trouble this would have caused and simply avoided the entire situation.

7 UNIVERSITY OF ARKANSAS

For the first time in my life, I was truly in charge of my own destiny when I went away to college at the University of Arkansas main campus in Fayetteville. There was no Mom to ask if I've done my homework. No Dad to tell me it was time for bed. No Mom to wake me up for school the next morning.

I spent many evenings talking with friends much too late or joining study sessions over pancakes at IHOP until 3am. Not surprisingly, I would end up sleeping until noon the next day and missing most or all of my classes.

I enjoyed the college environment and the amazing things Fayetteville had to offer, compared to my hometown. Unfortunately, with autism comes a reliance on habits, and I had formed those habits during early 80s summer nights listening to the radio until midnight and having a hard time waking up the next day for school. Now, with nobody to wake me up, and a little bit of depression settling in due to being away from family and most of my friends, the only part of my routine that was intact was staying up too late and sleeping in.

Time and time again, I paid dearly for my poor study habits. My first semester in college, I had a Calculus class. Had I applied myself better in high school, the class would have been easy. Surprisingly, I had zero fear walking up to and striking up a conversation with the most beautiful girl I had ever seen, who sat near me in the class. She agreed to meet me the next day in the library to study together. She told me there were three homework questions she couldn't figure out. Of course, I hadn't looked at them in advance. I tried to figure them out, but was as baffled as she was. When she realized I didn't have a clue about how to do the homework, and also had zero game, she politely excused herself and never spoke to me again.

8 DJ KEVIN KELLY

One day, my friend David and I were listening to a radio station that played country music, which we both enjoyed. I recognized one of the morning DJs, because he had been the nighttime DJ at a rock and roll station in Little Rock several years earlier. David realized that if school wasn't working out for me, I'd need a backup plan. He began gently guiding me towards a new possibility. First, he acknowledged how much I loved music and listening to my favorite DJs. Then he suggested that since school wasn't going so well for me that maybe I should get in touch with that DJ and see if he would talk to me about radio career possibilities. I agreed that it seemed like a good idea.

I called the station and actually got the DJ on the phone. He agreed to a meeting with me. During our conversation, I discovered that not only was he the morning host, but he was also the program director. That means he was in charge of all the on-air programming and the other DJs on the station, which was the top-rated station in town.

We had a great conversation and I learned a lot about radio in that hour. Just before I left, he said he might be able to find some work for me and asked me to send him a resume. I told him I'd never had a job before, so he said to just list some of my academic accomplishments. A few days later, I sent him the resume, and soon I was working part time doing what they referred to as "call out research" for the station! This was an interesting job. I sat in a production room where the DJs produced and recorded commercials during the daytime and called random people in the early evening to ask them what radio stations they listened to, and wrote down their responses. If they listened to us, I asked them if they'd mind listening to a few song snippets and rating the songs. Most people hung up on me, but a few were polite enough to complete the music survey. I had found something that made me happy!

One night, I was hanging out with the weekend overnight DJ and watching her work. Around 1 AM, I said something about how I'd love to be on the radio someday. She offered to let me actually be on the air for an hour of her show. She asked me what my radio name was going to be. I got nervous, and said I didn't know. Since I wasn't expecting to be on the air yet, I hadn't thought about it. She asked what my middle name was. I answered "Kelly." She looked at me for a moment, and said "you are now Kevin Kelly!" So, for the next hour, I was Kevin Kelly! I had never been so nervous or so excited! The excitement lasted until the next week, when I was in the office getting ready to do my call out research and I saw the program director. I began to feel guilty about being on the air without permission, so I confessed what had happened. I expected him to fire me. He thanked me for being honest with him and sternly told me to never do anything like that again without permission. The next day he called me at home to tell me the overnight weekend DJ was no longer with us, and asked if I'd like the job.

One day, I was walking down the hallway at the station, and I noticed that Michael Martin Murphey was walking towards me. He is most famous for the 1975 song "Wildfire", but he was one of the hottest country stars in the late 80s. I was so surprised to see him, I couldn't think of a single thing to say. I believe he was the first star I encountered in person. Many people with autism don't do well when their routine is disturbed. Seeing a famous musician walk past me in the hallway definitely was not in my routine!

For most of my life, when I became aware that I was going to talk with ANYONE besides normal friends, I would spend hours rehearsing the possible conversations and what things I might say. This applied to calling and asking a girl out on a date too. In the days before social media or cell phones, asking a girl out was either done in person or by calling a landline phone and asking whoever answered if you could speak with her. The funny thing is, of all the potential conversation topics I rehearsed in my head, they never seemed to play out that way in reality. The other person would always say something I hadn't considered, then I was stuck and had to wing it. Which I only became good at in my mid-forties.

I worked late nights mostly, which meant I was alone at the station for the most part. Just me and the music, and I liked working that way. I wasn't totally alone… there were the listeners, but they were invisible to me. I had a few "groupies" who called regularly. They weren't the kind of groupies you think of from movies though, because this was a country oldies station. Most of them were older men who simply enjoyed the music. I was slightly locally famous, but not famous enough for the young ladies to notice. There was one girl though, who was a cashier at a grocery store who was star struck because I was on the radio. We met through mutual friends. We hung out a few times, but nothing much ever came of that.

9 MY FIRST GIRLFRIEND

I worked for the radio station for a year, then moved back home for a while. One day, I went into a convenience store, and noticed a blonde girl in cowboy boots as I was walking out. One of us said something to the other, and before you know it, a date was set up. At this point in my life, I thought a pretty girl who paid attention to me was a girl I should be dating. I didn't have the interpersonal skills to realize I should take time to get to know her and find out if we were compatible or not. The fact that she noticed me was enough for my first real relationship to develop. And we dated for about a year and moved to Biloxi, Mississippi together before breaking up.

10 THE 1990'S – SO I GOT TO BE A RADIO STAR

In 1990, I was working at a legendary top 40 powerhouse radio station on the Gulf Coast. Great job for a person with autism as long as I stayed in the studio. But working for a top 40 station in a beach town meant I had to interact with people, not only on the telephone, but also in person at station appearances. I was not good at working the crowds, as I kept to myself as much as I could.

The first thing I noticed about working for a popular top 40 station was that we had a different audience than that country station had. I actually had female groupies and fans at this place! I also became slightly locally famous. I met several of those fans, and became friends with a few. Was invited to a listener's funeral. I went on a few random dates with some of them. Got more involved with a couple of them.

Even though I was young and had lots of energy, I needed something to keep me awake when the request lines stopped ringing around 3 or 4 am and I was getting sleepy. I didn't smoke, do drugs, or drink coffee like some of the other DJs. We didn't even have a vending machine, but there was a convenience store next door. The bad thing was, nobody was trusted with keys to the building and the doors automatically locked behind you when they closed. I had to make sure I had at least a four-minute-long song to run out of the control room, put something in the door to prop it slightly open, run next door, pick out a candy bar and root beer, pay for it, and return to my studio in time to start the next song with no dead air.

Fortunately, the girl who worked overnight at the gas station got to know me fairly quickly. If I found myself at the end of a long line to check out, looking nervous like I wasn't going to make it back in time, she'd call me to the front of the line and tell the person I was cutting in front of that I had to get back to my job next door. She was attractive and I soon figured out I could play a six- or seven-minute dance mix of a song to give me enough time to flirt with her a little. I thought she was interested in me, so I was about to ask her out one night, until she said something about going on a motorcycle ride with one of my coworkers. Oh well. One more instance of not reading the woman's body language correctly.

I was beginning to realize that I was having a tough time adapting to the work world. People with autism have to not only learn a new job, but also learn how to navigate the workplace, filled with unwritten social rules that we don't understand. For instance, I arrived to do an overnight shift on the AM station one night, and I noticed the main lights were off in the FM studio and the mood lights were on. The morning man and the evening guy were both in there with two beautiful women and champagne glasses in everyone's hands. The morning guy was also the program director, so nobody got in trouble for that.

I was on a date on a different evening and lost track of time. I was supposed to be on the air at 2am and found a clock when it was 1:45. I didn't have time to take the girl home, so I brought her to the radio station. She sat in the guest announcer chair and whenever I wasn't talking, we were kissing. The overnight announcer on the other station told the DJ who came on after her that I had a hot girl in the studio, used the wrong verbiage to explain that we had been kissing, and the story changed into something X-rated as it spread around. Two days later, I was called into the program director's office where he yelled at me for having a girl in the studio. I finally explained that we only kissed and he calmed down once he believed me. I was so shocked to be yelled at about this that I didn't think to call him out for doing the same thing another night.

11 HOW MY FUTURE FATHER-IN-LAW INTRODUCED ME TO MY FUTURE WIFE

From one relationship to another, the common thread was the woman chose to pursue me and I quickly allowed myself to be caught. In the spring of 1993, I accepted a job as program director of the newest radio station in town, which was also the lowest rated station in town. My goal was to turn it around and make it successful and parlay that into a job in a bigger city. One day, I got out of the elevator and was walking down the hallway when the door to the radio station opened, and a middle-aged man I didn't know began slowly backing out into the hallway. I heard the midday guy (also my best friend) telling the man "Kevin Kelly is the guy you need to see, sorry he's not here yet." I froze and realized that if someone was looking for me at this radio station it couldn't be good news! I turned around and started walking quickly towards the elevator. I was about to turn the corner and safely disappear into the still waiting elevator when I heard Steve's voice calling me. "Kevin! There he is!" So, reluctantly, I turned around again and greeted the man and asked what I could do to help him.

 The stranger explained that he was retiring to the area and his family would be moving with him. His daughter was a DJ in Ohio and would be looking for a job, so he'd appreciate it if I could reach out to her. He gave me the request line number for her radio station and I agreed to give her a call. I waited until she'd been on the air for an hour and then dialed the number. "Hello, Kiss Country" said the voice on the other end. I introduced myself and said her dad had visited my station and told me she'd be moving to Biloxi soon and looking for a job, so I wanted to reach out and see if I could help her in any way. I paused, and there was silence on the other end. After a full five seconds, I heard her take a deep breath, then she started yelling. "I TOLD HIM that I'm not moving to any g*d**** f***ing Mississippi!" My mouth was hanging open and I was now the silent one. Any normal non-autistic person would have said the obvious thing "sorry to bother you, goodbye!" and hung up. I continued to hold the phone with my mouth open not knowing what to do. She finally apologized and we talked for half an hour. Fast forward three weeks later, I was on my way to Ohio for the first time ever for a weekend visit. A few months later, she was working for my old radio station. A few more months later, we got married.

12 THE WORLD'S MOST FAMOUS BEACH

Before I knew anything about autism, I realized that I had one of the symptoms: an "inflexible adherence to routine." I discovered this in 1997 while living in Daytona Beach. I was hungry and decided to place an order with my favorite sandwich wrap shop down the street. I picked up the phone and dialed the number. A guy answered the phone quickly and said "Astros, we'll be there in ten minutes" and slammed the phone down. I stood there with a bewildered look on my face, and my (at the time) wife asked me what happened. When I told her, she said to call back. When I did, the same guy answered again and sounded annoyed. He simply asked "What's wrong?" I replied that he hadn't taken my order. He said, "you want a build-your-own wrap with turkey, extra cheese, and mayo only, right?" I said "Yes." He replied "We'll be there in ten minutes" and slammed his phone down again. Ten minutes later, there was a knock on the door. When I opened the door and the delivery guy saw me, he burst out laughing. He said "Sorry dude, but we've been slammed the last two hours. We have Caller ID, and you order the same thing every time, so to save time my manager just answered and said we'll be there in ten minutes." We all laughed. Until that moment, I had no idea that I was so predictable.

13 THE 2000'S - OHIO

My wife's radio station changed formats to Spanish, and she was offered a transfer to either Jacksonville (an hour north of us) or to Columbus, Ohio. I loved the warm weather of Florida, but she missed having seasons, so she took the job in Columbus. We moved in October 1999. I hated the cold weather that soon arrived, and spent the final six years of our marriage trying to figure out how to move us back to Florida. Ironically, she returned to Daytona Beach for a while and I ended up staying in Columbus.

14 COWORKERS

Social rules associated with coworkers and bosses are very difficult to understand for someone with autism. The boundaries are different from everyday social or family interactions. This makes finding a compatible job difficult.

After moving to Columbus, it took several years for me to find a workplace where I fit in and could thrive. One of the places that didn't work out for me was a local telecom company. One day during new hire training, I was taking my time leaving the training room for lunch. One of my fellow trainees approached me in the otherwise empty room and asked if we could talk. She confided in me that she had just been through a breakup and asked if she could talk with me about it. I was nervous and didn't know what to say. I couldn't make eye contact with her. I suggested she talk with our trainer because she seemed like someone who would be good at talking about relationships. The girl teared up and said she agreed with me, and walked away. She never spoke to me again in the short time I was there. As soon as she walked away, I regretted turning her away. Unfortunately, people with autism are good at talking "at" someone, not talking "with" them.

15 KIDS AND AUTISM

Things have a way of coming full circle. As I mentioned earlier, I always had a tough time relating to kids, even when I was one. I always had an easier time bonding with adults. My therapist says that's because adults are more adept at dealing with the personality quirks of a person with autism. When I had my own kids, it was just as difficult. Kids are unpredictable.

Sometimes kids will be unpredictable to such an extreme that you know something is wrong. One of our children had numerous behavioral issues that eventually led to a diagnosis of autism in 2007. As parents, we were not able to agree on the best way to handle these medical issues on the way to the diagnosis, which had laid bare our incompatibility in the relationship. There were many disagreements and arguments that really took a toll on us. We divorced in 2005 and I had moved on to my next relationship by the time of the diagnosis.

I decided that I wanted to learn more about autism to understand what my child was going through, so I did a bit of research and purchased a book written by a man who had been diagnosed with autism as an adult. As I read the first couple of chapters, I saw only a little bit of my child in the author's words. But I saw a lot of myself in those words. With each chapter I read, I began to identify more and more closely with what I was reading. By the end of the book, I decided that I must be autistic also! So, I bought another copy and took it over to my ex's place the next weekend when I was picking up my kids. I presented the book and told her she had to read it because it made me believe that I was autistic as well. She said, "Thank God, you finally figured it out!" Then she told me she didn't need to read the book because she knew what autism was like after living with both of us for so long. Thanks to my child's diagnosis, I realized at the age of 39 that I probably was autistic.

16 THE 2010'S – EXPANDING HORIZONS

By the turn of the new decade, my life was going a little smoother career-wise. I'd been at my job for over four years, the longest I'd worked anywhere. But I still didn't have a diagnosis or any healing modalities, and I was struggling both socially and romantically.

17 EXPLORING WITH MY PHOTOGRAPHY GROUP

I have never liked going places alone, especially places I am unfamiliar with. I joined a photography group at the beginning of 2010, and started going to their Meetup events. This started getting me out of my comfort zone and stretching my limits a little bit. At first, I felt uncomfortable going to the restaurant meeting room in Dublin where we gathered once a month. Before long, we were taking field trips to Metro Parks to photograph wildlife and wildflowers. I was stepping further and further outside my box and finally exploring some of the other suburbs of the city where I'd lived for a decade.

Eventually, I decided that if I wanted to enjoy living in

Columbus, I needed to become acquainted with the downtown area. I finally mustered the courage to join the group for a photo walk around the Short North, an artsy neighborhood just north of downtown Columbus. There was a lot of traffic and not many parking lots like you'd find in the suburbs. So, I drove around until I figured out where to park safely. I enjoyed walking around the neighborhood and exploring the shops. I decided I'd like to spend more time around this neighborhood.

18 NEW YORK, NEW YORK

For many years, I had wanted to visit New York City. But every time someone suggested I go, I always said that I wanted to go with a native New Yorker. Something about the size of the city just scared me, and I had quite a bit of anxiety about it.

For two years, I dated a woman whose parents lived in New Jersey. That finally afforded me the opportunity to go into the city with someone who was almost a native New Yorker. We took a train in from New Jersey. The biggest problem we encountered was being in a subway station and not knowing which way to go... Eventually, a man who had a couple of minutes to spare stopped and asked us where we were trying to go, and told us how to get to the right platform.

The surprising part of this for me was that the city didn't overwhelm my senses. Just a few years earlier, I would almost have a panic attack from walking into a shopping mall in Columbus. Now here I was walking down 5th Avenue in Manhattan with no problems. Just knowing a little bit about autism seemed to help me quell my anxiety a bit so I could enjoy exploring a new place.

19 SWIMMING LESSONS

My girlfriend thought it was crazy that a grown man couldn't swim, so she offered to teach me. Every time I got into our apartment complex pool, I immediately sank to the bottom. Finally, I convinced her I needed something to keep me from going under. We went to the store and found pool noodles! We bought two, one for each arm. These did not really work as expected, and she soon abandoned the project.

Later on, her mother would tell her that not everyone can float. So, I simply assumed that I was just not ever going to be able to swim.

Even later on, I would learn that all the sensations of being in the water and having nothing solid to support me were the issues I needed to conquer. I would need to find a specialized swim class for autistic people.

20 DAD'S PASSING

Dad passed away in September of 2011. This was a devastating thing for me to go through. He had survived every medical issue including a serious heart attack, so I just couldn't imagine he wouldn't recover from a stroke.

I began to see a minister for counseling after Dad suffered the stroke. My minister's mother was also in the final weeks of her life, so it was an immense act of kindness for him to help me.

He loaned me a book about grief. We discussed it a couple of weeks later. I told the minister that I felt misled by the book. The author's premise was that the choices we make as adults that don't serve our best interest are usually rooted in something traumatic or something missing from our childhood.

I then told him that my childhood was perfect. I grew up in a small town, my mom was a stay-at-home mom, and my dad was always off somewhere working... As my voice trailed off, the minister slowly cocked his head to one side as he saw the look of awareness wash over my face.

The grief I experienced was that my dad was never around, and now it was too late to make up for lost time. The minister helped me realize that I needed to forgive Dad for doing the best he could to support the family by being off at a job site. Forgiveness would be critical to my healing process.

21 FIRST CONCERT ALONE

The first concert I saw alone was by accident. I got into an argument with a girlfriend about something while we were on the way to see a free outdoor show in June of 2012. She was driving, and took me back to my car.

On my way home, I decided to go to the show anyway. I drove downtown, parked, and sat on a park bench near the pizza vendors, away from the crowd. I felt very uncomfortable, but enjoyed the show a reasonable distance away from the crowd.

22 THE LAW OF ATTRACTION

If you are socially awkward, you will probably draw some other socially awkward people into your life. Ok, let's be honest... your life could at some point become FILLED with socially awkward people. I used to say that I attracted "entertaining" people into my life. Someone should have pointed out to me that there is a difference between people who are "entertaining" and people who have mental or emotional issues.

One time, I matched with a woman on a dating site, but no conversation developed. A month later, she messaged me out of the blue and asked me to take her to a summer community festival to see a reggae band. She said I'd have to pick her up because her car was having problems. The band turned out to be really good, but she turned out to be "entertaining."

She seemed to be having a fun time with me, and we ended up at a nearby bar after the festival closed for the night. The more she drank, the more she became determined to talk to everyone in the bar, dragging me along with her from one group of people to the next. Most of them just ignored her as she tried to butt in to their conversations.

But the final group she approached in the bar welcomed us in. Two young and attractive Russian couples. My date ended up making out with one of the hot Russian girls in the front window of the bar while the rest of us continued chatting and enjoying the show. My date noticed that the diners in the restaurant across the street were watching her and the Russian girl, so she said "you want something to look at?" and proceeded to pull up her shirt and flash them.

For those of you keeping score at home, I would have been better off if I'd left when she started annoying the first of the patrons at the bar. That $100 bar tab would have been less, and I wouldn't have wasted the next 29 nights going through similar embarrassments.

Years later, I would discover the "problem with her car" was that she had wrecked it while driving under the influence.

23 MEDITATION FAMILY

There was one good thing to come out of the date with the festival girl. Dancing in front of the stage at the reggae show was an older man wearing only cut off shorts and a long beard. She practically dragged me over to introduce me to him. The band was so loud, neither of us could hear her introduction, so we simply smiled at each other, then she and I walked away.

For the next two weeks, she kept insisting that I find and follow him on social media. I finally gave in and sent him a friend request, which he soon accepted. I noticed he posted from time to time about meditations at his home. Eventually, I began attending his meditation group and found that I liked his style. I had found a new circle of friends!

24 YOGA FAMILY

I started dating a yoga teacher in summer of 2013 and I was a little bit curious what yoga was like. I heard people talking about it all the time. Eventually I asked her to show me what yoga was all about, and she led me through my first yoga flow.

I enjoyed the experience, so I asked if we could do yoga together regularly. She said no. Her practice was private, her own solitary experience. She then encouraged me to find a class somewhere, so I decided to try a class at the yoga studio where she practiced. I went there a few times without her and enjoyed the practice. The teacher played rock music which made it feel like an exercise class.

Not long after I started doing yoga, we broke up in the spring of 2014. I didn't want to bump into her, so I stopped going to her yoga studio. One of my friends found out about the breakup and suggested that I try a class at her favorite yoga studio. When I did, I found this teacher had a very spiritual practice and didn't play rock and roll music. Her music of choice was called kirtan. I instantly knew I had found my new yoga home.

25 MY AUTISM DIAGNOSIS

Following the demise of these relationships, an ex-girlfriend strongly urged me to see a therapist. I hesitated, so she set up the appointment for me. I finally received my autism diagnosis in the spring of 2014.

At this point, I was able to go back and reevaluate all the major life decisions that previously hadn't made sense through the new lens of the diagnosis. Once I understood how my brain worked differently than most people, it was easy to see how I had reasoned all the decisions. Subsequent therapy would help me see new possibilities and make future decisions differently.

My minister told me that my diagnosis was a gift, because it allowed me to understand myself better. He suggested that in future relationships I should ask for feedback because my assumption making mechanism was broken. If a woman were to tell me to take things slow, I should ask for clarification.

It felt good to finally have answers to the questions that had haunted me all my life. Questions about why I didn't fit in, why I made choices that led to poor outcomes so often.

I soon learned that my minister would be retiring. I was happy for him, but sad that I wouldn't be able to see him or hear his healing words on future Sundays. Fortunately, I still had my therapist.

26 FIRST CONCERT TRIP TO CHICAGO ALONE

In July of 2014, I stepped even further out of my box, by driving from Columbus to Chicago to see my favorite band The Kings. They are a "one hit wonder" band from Toronto with a lot of great songs. I didn't even book a hotel room before I left! I really flew by the seat of my pants this time!

I made good time and arrived a couple of hours early, but went straight to the venue, wary of rush hour traffic. They had a rooftop patio, so I went up and had a sandwich before the performance room opened.

Sadly, when I walked back down to the performance room, I discovered that a few people had entered the bar and claimed the two tables in front of the stage. I had to settle for the second table back, about ten feet from the band.

I mentioned to the server that I had driven from Columbus, and the guys who sat at the table next to me began talking with me. We were each holding down tables with four chairs and they weren't expecting guests, so I asked if I could join them and free up my table for other fans. They welcomed me to join them and I had a great conversation with them. We remain social media friends to this day.

The plan to find a hotel after I left the concert almost turned into a huge problem. I knew that Lollapalooza was happening the following week at Grant Park. What I didn't realize was that all the people who set up the event arrived in Chicago a week in advance to do the set up and had taken up every hotel room in the city. After I left the bar at 1:30am, I spent the next hour searching hotel websites on my phone trying to find an empty room. I finally found two options: a $400 room in one of the high rises downtown, or an $80 room 45 minutes away in Schaumburg. Coincidentally, I was meeting a coworker in Schaumburg the next day for lunch, so I chose that one.

27 FIRST MOVIE ALONE

The first movie I saw by myself was "Avengers: Age of Ultron" in May of 2015. I entered the theater and put on the 3D glasses and enjoyed the movie, even though I was surrounded by strangers. Thanks to the earlier efforts to step outside my box, and the yoga and meditation, I was able to center myself and be present to enjoy the movie without feeling self-conscious that I was alone.

28 MOVING DAY 2016

Moving is an activity that's always overwhelmed me. Having to pack up everything I own, move it all, then unpack and set up a new place had always been more than I could handle alone. This time was no exception.

I was moving with somewhat short notice. I had been on maybe two dates with a woman who offered to help me pack. When she showed up and realized I'd packed nothing, she was a little worried. She took charge and helped me get around half of my stuff packed.

The next day, my other friends arrived, and they helped box the rest of my things. They all gave me grief over this for a long time. Somehow, the new woman didn't run away, and we casually dated off and on for the next two years.

My therapist helped me understand that moving is a

disruption to my normal routine, and that's hard to handle.

29 ADULT RELATIONSHIPS

A couple of years later, I asked for and received detailed feedback from that woman following the end of our relationship.

One of the main reasons she thought we didn't work out was the way I related important stories to her in a "just the facts" manner, like a news reporter might have done. She felt that I didn't seem to show any emotion.

She brought up a conversation we had in a park a year or so earlier, where I explained all the skeletons in my closet. To save time, I told her in rapid succession about my fairly recent (at the time) autism diagnosis, my previous failed relationships, and how the diagnosis helped me understand why, at the time, I thought those were good relationships to be in, when most of the women were clearly not compatible with me.

She mentioned another time that I had told her my son was in the hospital in Chicago. Again, I explained the facts of his medical condition without showing the emotions I was feeling inside.

By sharing my story and only relating the facts, I came across to her as callous and uncaring. I totally missed her non-verbal expressions of surprise that I wasn't giving off the normal non-verbal cues showing that I was bothered by the things I was sharing with her.

A trained therapist who knew how to converse with someone with autism might have asked probing questions like, "and how did you feel about that?" at various points in my stories. But she wasn't a therapist, so she experienced shock at what she perceived as my lack of emotion.

    She didn't realize that inside, I was hurting and upset. I just didn't know how to show it.

PART TWO

SELF HELP GUMBO

This is the part of my story where the healing modalities come into play, so we'll pivot and cover them in this section of the book.

I recently read an article that said one in five Americans live with anxiety at any given point in time. If you are autistic, your coping mechanisms may really struggle when you feel anxiety.

Fortunately, I have discovered several methods of reducing or eliminating anxiety. The magical thing about using multiple coping strategies at the same time is that they reinforce and magnify each other.

If you try one of these things and it doesn't work for you, you can always substitute something else. Your path to growth might end up being different from mine, but these are still good activities to begin with. Enjoy and trust the process, and don't become overwhelmed!

These activities may be new to you, and new things can feel scary to someone on the spectrum. But it'll be ok. Here's the secret to success… The biggest thing you can do to begin to transcend autism (or anything else you feel is holding you back) is to step outside your box. Doing new things and experiencing new experiences actually rewires your brain, establishing new neural pathways and creating new possibilities for your life! There is plenty of research that proves these tools work!

30 YOGA

Yoga is one of my favorite things to do. It is a framework and spiritual discipline that harmonizes spirit and body. The word yoga is actually derived from an ancient Sanskrit word that means "to yoke" or "to unite." My yoga practice enables me to exercise my body and clear my mind. It also helps me focus on being present in the moment. A yoga practice can also incorporate other healing modalities such as meditation.

So, what are the benefits of yoga, you ask? I thought you'd never ask! The yoga poses and movements are designed to strengthen and tone the body in the following ways:

- Holding a pose for a short time can strengthen your muscles.
- Standing poses can increase your balance.
- Movement can increase your flexibility.
- Seated twists can help relieve back pain.
- Restorative yoga can help reduce arthritis symptoms.
- A slower practice before bed can help you get to sleep faster and wake feeling more rested.
- A power flow practice in the morning can energize you and set a great mood for the day.
- Yoga can reduce your stress levels.
- Participating in a yoga class can provide a new social connection and support network.

You will learn breath work that synchronizes with the movements. When you are focused on the breathwork that goes with the poses, you will find that your mind isn't wandering. You aren't thinking about the grocery shopping you need to do later, or the business deal you are working on, or the family issue you might be having. You are focused on your breath and movements and nothing else. This is the first step towards "being in the moment" and experiencing mindfulness.

I've heard of people who don't want to do yoga because they think it's some weird kind of religion. Yoga is an ancient practice that originated in India as a way to exercise, breathe, relax, and even meditate.

The original students of yoga were practitioners of Hinduism, Buddhism, and Jainism. But yoga is available to anyone.

Yoga can be both a spiritual and physical practice, but it is not a religion.

Spirituality is the personal relationship between a person and their deity or god. When you do yoga, you aren't being forced to worship any particular deity. Worship is not the point, so it doesn't matter what your religion is or isn't.

Religion is the group study or worship of that deity or god. So, yoga isn't a religion unless your teacher is preaching.

31 MEDITATION

Meditation is a way to let go and sit in stillness. Meditation can leave you feeling calm, clear, happy, and stress free. This is scientific fact, based on brain chemistry and a concept called neuroplasticity. Stress releases chemicals in your body and brain that are unhealthy, along with increasing the number of bad connections between neurons. Meditation releases happy chemicals into your body and brain and increases the number of good connections between neurons.

Meditation can lead to personal and spiritual growth. My meditation guide says meditation is "sitting with God." It can be a very intense and personal thing, depending on the person. It is also super easy to do.

To meditate, you can simply sit alone in a quiet room and close your eyes for a few minutes. Focus your attention on your breath. Breathe in and count slowly to three. Hold for one second. Breathe out and count slowly to three. Hold for a second at the bottom. Then repeat, as many times as you like.

At first, you might have a hundred thoughts floating around your head. As you meditate more often, you'll eventually find the number of thoughts drops to maybe 90. Close your eyes and focus on your senses. What do you feel on your skin? What sounds do you hear? Is there a trace of light visible through your closed eyelids? The more you focus on your senses, the less ability your brain will have to think about grocery lists and other distractions. Down to 60 thoughts now.

I picture my mind like an empty house. If a thought enters, I imagine it to be like a bird that flew in through an open window. I notice it, acknowledge its existence, then watch as it flies across the room, then out an open window on the other side of the room.

Another way to visualize this is to imagine your brain is a computer and your thoughts are the operating system.

Once you realize your brain and your thoughts are two separate things, it becomes a lot easier to control your thoughts and put them on pause.

32 MINDFULNESS

Mindfulness is one of the results of meditation. Mindfulness is about being aware. Living in the moment. Being present. Which are difficult things to do for an autistic person.

The past exists for reference purposes only. Living in the

past causes you to feel depression. On the other hand, worrying excessively about the future usually causes anxiety. You live in the current moment, so tune into your senses. This is the only moment that matters. Making the best decisions in any given current moment will ensure you have the best future possible. So, feel the current moment. Embrace mindfulness.

Now I'm going to let you in on a couple of secrets. You are cluttering your mind with background noise all the time, and don't even realize it!

The first change I'm going to suggest you make can lower your stress dramatically. Next time you have to go somewhere, try to get in your car a couple of minutes early. Sit there quietly for a minute and just focus on your breath. Breathe in slowly through your nose as you count to three, then hold the breath for one second, then breathe out to the count of three. Hold for one second, then repeat the process a couple of times. Focus on your senses. If it's sunny, feel the sun on your skin. Notice the temperature. Notice any sounds coming from outside. When you are ready, turn on your car. What happens next? Most likely, your favorite radio station or music from your phone starts blaring. Do yourself a favor and switch it off. Yes, turn off the music in your car. Try driving to your destination with no music on. Alone with your thoughts. Try to be more aware of your surroundings. If someone cuts you off, don't road rage. Just focus on your breathing and cut them some slack. Maybe they are having a bad day, a family member might be sick or something. Say to yourself, "They are human, they suffer." Show them compassion. They are probably in a huge hurry, in a bad mood, with music blaring. You are cool, calm, and collected.

Make this mindset a habit.

The second thing I'm going to suggest happens when you return home from that trip. What do most people do when they come home in the evening? Grab a remote and turn on the TV. How often do you have a television on just for background noise? Don't do it this time. Leave it off. Be alone with your thoughts for a while. Read a book instead. Take out a notebook or journal and do some writing. Dust off the guitar in your basement and play some music. Do anything creative instead of mindlessly consuming someone else's commercial content.

33 JOURNALING

Journaling can be helpful in many ways. Writing out your thoughts, fears, dreams, or problems can give you a starting point for working through these things. To begin with, journaling requires mindfulness. Then once done, seeing your thoughts on paper can spur you to begin to address the issues. You also get a written point of reference you can return to later on to measure your progress.

One tip is to journal before going to bed. Take time out to reflect on your day, then write some relevant things in your journal. Also, think of the things you need to do the next day. Write down those things in a "to-do" list. Picture your mind as being clear since you've dumped all this info onto the pages of your journal. Put down the journal and pen, turn off the light, do a quick breathing exercise or meditation, and drift peacefully off to sleep.

34 COUNSELING

Counseling or therapy is a fabulous process to help you work things out in your head. The hardest part for me was finding a therapist that I liked and vibed with. I had a few sessions each with a couple of therapists before a random suggestion led me to the perfect one.

They'll probably have you spend the first few sessions explaining your current situation and dilemmas. You'll get help with any urgent issues. Then they'll deep dive into your past in order to try and figure out why you have made the decisions that led you to the current place.

Last, your therapist will ask you questions to gently guide your thinking into normal, healthy decision-making processes.

My original individual therapy goals were to improve my self-awareness and self-acceptance, to establish coping mechanisms, and to improve my interpersonal relationships. As time has gone by, I've become very self-aware and have become adept at cultivating meaningful relationships.

35 PEER SUPPORT

Talking with someone else on the autism spectrum can be an important resource. Other autistic people have their own experiences that they could share with you, if they are willing of course. Most neurotypical people aren't quite sure how to interact with an autistic person. Having a peer to give you advice on interacting with schools, law enforcement, employers, and other specific groups that everyone encounters from time to time can be an incredible help.

36 PHYSICAL ACTIVITY

Research shows that regular physical activity provides many benefits for people, including those of us who are autistic.

- Motor skills development
- Social functioning and interactions
- Emotional regulation
- Physical and muscular strength
- Weight loss and regulation
- Increased energy
- Overall happiness

Any exercise gets your body moving and creates serotonin and endorphins that make you feel better. These benefits are especially important for someone who is autistic.

37 SPEND TIME OUTDOORS IN NATURE

Being in nature causes similar benefits to meditation, from calmness to joyfulness. Breathing fresh air and hearing sounds of nature can reduce stress and increase your joy and happiness. It doesn't matter if you walk through a city park, stroll through a neighborhood garden, hike in a remote national park, or visit a beach and listen to the waves crash against the shore. Any exposure to nature provides tangible benefits.

38 GRATITUDE

Giving thanks shouldn't be something we only do the fourth Thursday of November, at least in the United States. An attitude of gratitude will serve you any day of the year! My children have noted that I had a somewhat pessimistic worldview before I found yoga and these other healing modalities. I actually credit gratitude with a large part of my change to a happy worldview.

The woman who introduced me to yoga had a tradition every November where she posted a "thankfulness blog" each day of that month. Beginning November 1, she would share on social media one thing she was thankful about. The next day, she would post a second thing, and so on and so forth. The only rule to the 30-day project was that she wouldn't repeat something. This required her to come up with 30 separate and distinct things for which she was thankful.

I decided to adopt this idea, and initially found it difficult to think of something every day. One day, I was thankful for my snow boots when we got an especially heavy snowfall early in the month. There were days I didn't post on time, because I had to think for an extra day to come up with something.

But a curious thing happened... by the end of the month, I wasn't posting just before midnight after worrying all day about what to post. I was posting in the middle of the day, and struggling to choose between three or four different positive things that I'd experienced. Just four weeks and I was finding joy and gratitude all throughout my day!

39 POSITIVE SELF-TALK

Even though you are becoming comfortable in your own skin alone with your thoughts, you might notice some negative self-talk drifting in. How many times has the inner voice inside your head said one of these things:

- "I don't know how I can..."
- "I'll never be able to…"
- "I'm not smart enough…"
- "I'm not pretty enough…"

"I'm not this, I'm not that…" That's negative self-talk. Where did that get started? I believe it started when we were children, the first time someone told you that you weren't good enough for something you wanted. Or maybe you, like me, were bullied in school. Maybe your parents compared you unfavorably to a sibling.

For many years, I thought these things were just built into the bedrock of our personalities, far too deep in our mental computer code to root them out. I thought all we could do is acknowledge the presence of these incorrect negative thoughts and just learn to work around them. Now I know that we CAN root them out!

While we don't want to live in or dwell in the past, our memories ARE there for reference purposes. Let me note that if the memories you are dealing with are very traumatic or triggering, you will want to do this next step under the guidance of a trained counselor, therapist, or psychologist.

If you are good to continue, take that memory of your

childhood out of storage and examine it. See yourself as that little boy or girl who was too young to fully understand what was happening or how to process the situation. For me, I can see young Kevin being taunted by another boy for being too skinny. When I was a little boy, I didn't know how to handle this. Today I know that it doesn't matter what my body type is, I am just as worthy as anyone else. I'm a strong, attractive, desirable man. Nobody can take that away from me. And I will no longer give up any of my personal happiness to stupid words said by ghosts from the past.

Even after you deal with the things that caused you to doubt yourself, negative self-talk might still creep in from time to time. The next time you hear something negative floating around your brain or coming out of your mouth, make a mental note of it. Try and catch yourself doing it a few times. Once you are good at noticing it in real time, you can correct it. "I don't know how to do this." The problem is, you DO know how to do things. "I'll never be able to accomplish a task." You ARE able to do it. "I'm not smart enough to get into that school." You ARE smart enough. "I'm not pretty enough to date that person." You ARE pretty enough. You have just convinced yourself that you aren't. Maybe you are trying to accomplish something that really isn't a good idea. Maybe you just haven't thought it through enough to have the answer. But you are a fabulous person who can accomplish great things, once you decide that you deserve to do them.

Whatever the situation, the next time you feel that you are about to trash talk yourself, stop and rephrase the sentence in a positive way. If you hear your mind say "I don't know how to solve this problem," spin it positive and say "I will find a way to solve this problem." Then figure out how to do what you just told yourself you are going to do. Ask for help if necessary. Make the positive statement true and find a way to solve the problem.

Your brain is wired to do what you want it to do. You don't believe me? Ask your brain what is two plus two? Right, the answer is four. You thought it before you read it. Your brain gives you answers when you ask for them. It stores information and believes what you tell it. So, tell your brain positive things about yourself and stop telling your brain negative things about yourself. It'll take a little while to undo the effects of all the years of saying bad things about yourself. But slowly over time, you'll notice subtle differences. One day, you'll notice that you ALWAYS say good things about yourself. And why shouldn't you? You should be your own best cheerleader!

40 AFFIRMATIONS

A further step in positive self-talk is to use affirmations. These are powerful declarative sentences stating that something that enhances your sense of security and competency is true. "I am safe." "I am loved."

If you don't feel particularly safe or loved, then modify the affirmation slightly by adding "these days" to the end. "I feel safer these days." "I am loved more these days." Maybe you don't feel safe all the time, but it can be true in one moment. "These days" modifies the affirmation and makes it true at times.

Say the affirmations again and again and you will find you begin to believe in what you are saying. You will also find the affirmation begins to become your new reality. Your brain will automatically seek situations where the affirmations become true more and more of the time.

41 DECLUTTERING

Without even realizing it, you've decluttered your mind with the previous activities. Now it's time to declutter your physical world! Decluttering your home and work spaces is very important. Clutter is a distraction, and the last thing any of us need is distractions. It's hard to get important stuff done when there are distractions around. You should start by choosing one area at home and one at work.

It took me several years and the help of several people, but I finally finished my decluttering project. It is such a relief to be able to find anything I need whenever I need it!

Ask a trusted friend to help you with this project if necessary. You can also find books and videos online from any number of decluttering experts.

42 POSTURE

Good posture is far more important than most people realize. Your posture is a reflection of how you feel about yourself. It also influences how you feel about yourself.

If you don't feel great, you might walk with your head down, staring at the ground in front of you as you walk. Don't do that. Stand up straight and tall with your shoulders back.

This is one of the first things you'll hear in a yoga class when you do mountain pose. This posture opens your shoulders and makes you feel open instead of closed. Look ahead with a light smile on your face. Who wants to walk around with a frown on their face? That's not fun! Greet people with a smile! Practice in the mirror if you need to. You are a happy person. Let the people you run into today see how happy you are.

43 COMMUNICATION

You have to learn to communicate with people. Being a radio DJ was a great job for me because I am creative with words. But being a DJ is one way communication.

To be in service to other people, one must be a good listener. I adopted a policy of "talking with" someone, as opposed to "talking to" them. It's a subtle shift in mindset, but it reminds you that talking is a collaborative adventure. If you are talking "with" someone, you are much less likely to be talking "at" them. People like intimate conversations, not aloof lectures.

Communication experts and coaches will often say to listen with the intent to understand, not with the intent to reply. If you are using all your mental horsepower thinking of what you are going to say next, then you don't have any bandwidth to hear what the other person is saying. Remember, communication is sharing BOTH ways.

44 CHOOSE YOUR FRIENDS WISELY

You might ask what your choice of friends has to do with anything. Everything! I've heard it said many times that in every way you are the average of your five closest friends. In income, education, career success, love life, happiness.... And nearly every other measure. Think about it. People whose lives could be considered dumpster fires usually have friends who have messed up lives as well. College professors hang around other college professors. Billionaires hang around other billionaires. Movie stars, well, you get it by now, right?

Look around you. Does your friend group seem representative of the lifestyle you want to lead? If not, you might want to consider making changes in your circle.

Choosing friends is an art, not a science. But there are some guidelines you can follow to choose friends wisely. You've probably been treated less than kind by at least one person in the past. If you were asked to make a list of the things you would want in a new friend, you might list things like, "they should be honest" or "they should be respectful towards me." These are exactly the kind of qualities you should not only seek but REQUIRE from your friends. So, make that list of qualities you want in your next friend. Each quality you list should be non-negotiable, meaning, someone who doesn't fit the description can't be your friend. Write it like this: "My friend is honest (or whatever it is) because I'm honest." "My friend is respectful towards me because I am respectful towards them." "My friend is successful because I'm on the path to success." Write the list now. I'll wait.

Once you have completed the list of qualities in your next friend, make a separate list of the five people you spend the most time with. Take them one at a time and compare them against the qualities you wrote in your list. Ask yourself if this person fits each of the requirements you just listed for your ideal friend. If your current friends don't meet your non-negotiable criteria of being your friend, then I'd suggest you think about how much time you want to spend with them in the future. If you only want honest friends, would you allow someone around you that is sometimes dishonest? Nope. Not anymore.

If you commit to making friends that meet your list of non-negotiables, and weeding out the people who don't fit your requirements, you'll notice the quality of time spent with these new friends will be much better than the quality of time spent with the old friends. Unless you did a great job of choosing friends before. But let's face it. Most of us have friends who are "grandfathered in" and wouldn't make the cut if you just met them today. We all grow at different rates. Some people just sit and stagnate. Your group of friends will change and mature over time as you yourself change and mature. And that's ok.

Here's some new information I've come up with.... On a first date, I look for three things related to trust: consistency in behavior, compatibility, and respect for boundaries.

Consistency in behavior is a huge indicator for trust. Trust is established and grows as time goes by if the other person consistently does what they say they are going to do. Trust is broken if they do not do what they say they are going to do.

Compatibility... Most people on a date think "is this person compatible with me?" But I also ask myself "am I a compatible match for her?" Some people don't know what they are looking for, and they'll date you for a year before they figure out that you aren't it. To avoid that, I try to determine what the other person's dreams and goals are, and then I ask myself if I'm compatible with her vision of her future. If not, then it's probably not going to work out in the end.

I've spent a lot of time working on establishing clear boundaries in my mind of what I'm comfortable with. I know exactly what I want from a relationship, and I know exactly what

I have to offer back. If someone fails to respect my boundaries, or tries to talk me into letting them cross my boundaries without my consent, then we are not gonna work.

45 THE CUMULATIVE EFFECT

By now, it should be clear that all these things both build on one another and support one another. Any one of these activities when done alone will benefit someone. But if you do most or all of them, all the time, the results will be supercharged. If you change your thoughts to be more positive and self-supportive, then you will notice your feelings have changed. You are feeling happier now, so now you are behaving differently and doing new things. Different actions lead to different results. Suddenly your life has changed! You are a new person and enjoying a new and better life!

PART THREE

THE SWEETNESS OF MOMENTS

46 MY CURRENT EXPERIENCE OF LIFE

I'll try my best to summarize what my experience of life is like these days.

I've seen massive results in my life by applying all these healing techniques. Today, I'm much more flexible in my thinking compared with even five or ten years ago. The quality of my friendships has improved. This in turn has improved the quality of the interactions we have. I'm more self-aware and assertive regarding my needs. All this has caused me to become more confident. Then I attempt and subsequently accomplish bigger things.

Great things lie ahead for someone who follows the path I've described. A person on the path to Transcending Autism will experience the Sweetness of Moments. He or she now talks "with" people instead of talking "at" people.

47 THE 2020'S - PANDEMIC DRIVING

The defining event of the early 2020s will probably be the emergence of the coronavirus. The only thing I enjoyed about life during the pandemic was being able to work from home every day. I didn't have to drive 18 miles each way to work and back daily.

It takes people with autism a little longer than usual to process information. Not a useful situation when trying to navigate heavy city traffic. Looking both ways before turning left onto a street, I'm overstimulated with visual info, and sometimes have to look both ways again and again to make sure I didn't miss something.

For most of my adult life, I have planned my trips to avoid

having to turn left onto a busy street without a traffic light. I'm aware that some people with autism are actually unable to drive. I really felt relaxed driving on the rare moments when I went out during the height of the pandemic because there was so little traffic on the streets and freeways.

Since the return of traffic, I have been better able to handle left turns onto streets. Being present helps me better focus on the task at hand.

48 THE ATLANTIC OCEAN

I went on a vacation with my best friend and her family to Virginia Beach in the summer of 2020. By then, I knew that my issue with learning to swim is the overwhelming sensations of being in a large body of water. Since I have been able to hold my breath while letting water run down my face in the shower for quite some time, I decided it was time to go a short distance out into the water with a boogie board borrowed from the condo we stayed in. I noticed it was very buoyant. When a big wave came in, I pushed off the bottom with my feet and simply rode the wave.

One time, the wave swept me completely off my feet, and the boogie board was the only thing that kept me from going under. However, I was now laying on my back in the water, clutching the boogie board against my chest, floating and unable to get my feet planted back on the bottom. Although I didn't know what to do next, I didn't panic, I calmly asked for help. My friend pulled me closer to the beach where I could put my feet on the bottom and stand up. The sensations were still a bit overwhelming. I decided to consider swimming lessons in the future from a person with experience teaching autistic students.

49 MOVING DAY 2020

One of my biggest challenges in the past has been preparing to move from one home to another. The part of my brain that gets overwhelmed when too much information is coming in gets clogged up when I'm faced with having to prepare all my belongings to be moved and get them all packed in boxes.

But after all the work I've done on myself, I was finally able to accomplish a move (during a pandemic!) where almost all the preparation was done by myself over a two-week period.

I did such a good job packing, that nobody who helped got mad at me for failing to prepare! I was also able to put my new place together and make it functional (again, mostly by myself) in two weeks.

50 SWIMMING AND KAYAKING

In December of 2022, I used my passport for the first time on a Caribbean vacation. My best friend insisted that I take swimming lessons. "Come on Kevin, we are spending a week at the beach! If you drown, it'll ruin my vacation." So, we both searched and called around and found a swimming school with an opening. To my surprise, the instructor had taught an autistic family member to swim! She took me to a separate pool, away from the main pool, filled with 5-year-olds and was very patient. By the fourth lesson, I was able to kick from one end of the pool to the other, on my back and on my stomach.

I was happy to find the waves were very gentle at the beach. I was able to float on my back for the first time ever and the waves didn't even wash over me! I even tried snorkeling, but my mustache kept the face mask from making a proper seal and I kept getting water in my nose. But I did float and swim in the Caribbean! I also felt comfortable enough to get into a kayak for the first time in my life and paddled over a mile to another island and back.

51 FINAL THOUGHTS

This rest of the story is now up to you, the reader, to write. We each walk our own path of learning and healing, so we will each arrive at an awareness of the Sweetness of Moments that is just as individual as each of our lives tend to be. This awareness will continue to grow and change as time passes. As time goes by, I hope to hear your success stories! I wish you the best of luck in your journey of healing and growth!

www.ingramcontent.com/pod-product-compliance
Lightning Source LLC
Chambersburg PA
CBHW030225170426
43194CB00007BA/864